HOW TO WRITE A NONFICTION BOOK IN 12 HOURS

12

WRITE FASTER
WRITE BETTER

MARYANNA YOUNG

12

How to Write a Nonfiction Book in 12 Hours

Maryanna Young © 2018

Print ISBN: 978-1-61206-171-9
Audio Book ISBN: 978-1-61206-179-5

Book Production by Hannah Rhinehart and Jennifer Regner

For more information, visit AlohaPublishing.com

Published by

ALOHA
PUBLISHING

AlohaPublishing.com

Printed in the United States of America

For those of you who think you are too busy
to share your idea with the world.

CONTENTS

WHY THE 12-HOUR CONCEPT WORKS

A statistic that's been floating around the internet since 2002 says 81 percent of the population feels they have a book inside of them—and yet very few people actually write a book. Why? Because the publishing process is surrounded by mystery and confusion. For the past decade I have dedicated a big part of my life to helping anyone who has an idea and a vision for a book cut through the confusion.

Writing a book can take a year (or a decade!) if you want it to or if you are finding your own way to do it. But if you don't have the time or don't want to spend hundreds of hours writing and refining your work, you can do it much faster—and it may be a better book as a result.

Books created by individuals with the support of highly specialized publishing professionals like editors, designers, and proofreaders are changing the publishing industry. They have found that it is possible to publish a book with the highest quality in the industry without jumping through the literally dozens of hoops required when publishing was only possible through New York-based, traditional publishers.

Amazon distribution and the worldwide reach of the internet allow direct communication from authors to readers everywhere—in so many forms that didn't exist before these significant game-changing platforms were available.

This book is your first step in gaining clarity around publishing. It simply describes what to do and how to do it, and faster than you might think.

Some people think I am crazy when I say the core material for a book can be *completely written in 12-20 hours*. After working on hundreds of books for clients, I believe that even the most complex books will be better quality if they are written in a shorter amount of time. You may take up to 20 hours, and that's okay—but the process simply doesn't need to take a year or longer.

It might take a little more time than 12-20 hours to refine and polish, but writing fast to get your core ideas down is what makes writing better. Most of the authors I know have discovered that the best ideas are right at their fingertips. But you must pull them from your brain, heart, and soul and get them on "paper" if you want others to read them.

And for some, it's not actually writing but rather creating a good outline and then getting the ideas and stories out verbally that inspires the best writing and creativity.

More busy people could get great content out into the world if they utilized **three key techniques:**

1.   Write without editing, in short bursts, from a simple book outline.

2.   Utilize interview-style questions, record your work, and put in transcript form.

3.   Find a great editor or editorial team to help you put everything together.

You may dismiss this "focus and write quickly" method as questionable, but my challenge to you is to try it even if your mindset tells you it's impossible.

Some busy executives and celebrities hire ghostwriters and others to write for them—however, being involved in the outline and interview portion is still part of the process, regardless of who organizes the words in a document.

This 12-hour writing system can enable you to achieve more than you ever thought was possible.

What could you do if you dedicated 12 focused hours to something meaningful that could help you accomplish a lifelong goal and allow you to be seen as an authority?

HOUR 1

WHAT'S YOUR PURPOSE?

Determine why you are writing a book. Work to describe your concept in 7-15 words. Define and narrow your audience to start understanding your niche. Determine how writing your book merges with your business and personal *why*.

First Action Item for Hour One: Why does writing this book matter to you? Your reason and purpose have to be strong motivators or you will quit somewhere in the process. Your *why* can be because writing a book has been a lifetime dream, readers keep asking for information on the topic, or you have determined a book will grow your personal brand or business.

☐ **Second Action Item:** Determine how your book will impact your readers and make it a "must have" product.

Answer three questions to determine if your book idea could be a "must have" product*:

YES   NO

☐   ☐   1. Will your content help someone understand a concept and how to master it more simply and with more clarity than other products in the marketplace?

Readers are willing to pay you for creating this shortcut.

☐   ☐   2. Does your information accelerate the learning curve on your topic, saving the reader both time and money?

Readers are willing to buy your content if it helps them learn new skills with ease or organizes information in a clear way.

☐   ☐   3. Does your information give your reader a new perspective on your topic or help them know the steps to make a transformational change in their life?

Readers are willing to buy your content if it helps them improve their lives.

*If the answer to NONE of these is YES . . . go back to your research and align your book's content so the answer to *at least one* of these *will* be YES.

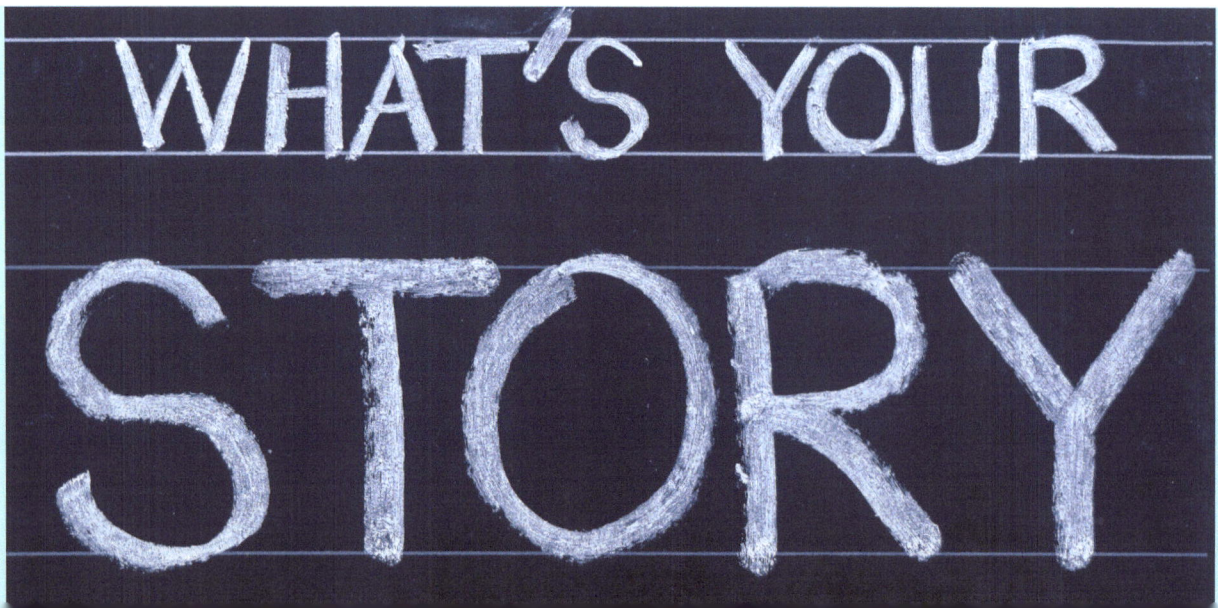

WHAT'S YOUR NICHE?
WHO IS YOUR AUDIENCE?

Research books written on similar topics and review their Tables of Contents. Determine the niche audience for your idea and begin developing the title and subtitle to address that audience.

First Action Item for Hour Two: Explore your topic on Amazon. Review the work of at least five thought leaders in your area of expertise. Determine how your ideas expand what already exists. Next, determine how to narrow your content to appeal to a specific audience who needs your information for a specific reason.

Dr. Cory Fawcett wrote the book, *The Doctors Guide to Smart Career Alternatives and Retirement* as one of three books in *The Doctor's Guide* series. By the time he got to this book, the third in the series, he had fully embraced this 12-hour method. The book was written for doctors who want to leave clinical practice to escape burnout, boredom, or frustration, or who are considering retirement. His secret to success with each book in his series was writing to a specific audience with a focused, problem-solving set of solutions for people in that audience and stage of life. His content was essential.

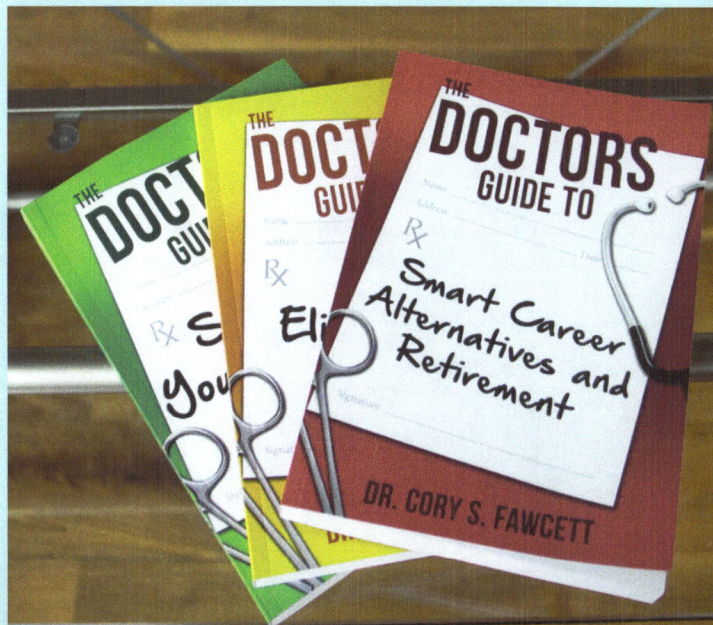

☐ **Second Action Item:** Think about your title and subtitle as you research. Review books in your niche on Amazon to make sure your title is unique. The title draws focus to a core idea and gets readers' attention, while the subtitle clarifies for readers what they will get from your book.

The title and the subtitle will be the most important words you write for your book.

The *title* should be one to five words long, memorable, and capture a key concept from your book. It should contain one or more keywords.

The *subtitle* can be up to 10 words or even longer, if you want to adopt the style of long, descriptive subtitles that some trending authors have used. The subtitle tells the reader what they will get from the book and oftentimes who the book will benefit. Keywords here are great, too.

Start with a working title and revisit it several times, modifying it until you get it right. You may go through several iterations before you find the right one. Often, it's easier to nail down the subtitle first, because that's more descriptive and is based on the book content.

When you think you have a good title, test it out on Amazon by using it as a search term to see what kind of books your "company" on screen would be. If you don't like what you see or none of those books are in your genre or niche . . . keep working.

Examples of good titles and subtitles:

- *Daring Greatly: How the Courage to Be Vulnerable Transforms the Way We Live, Love, Parent, and Lead* by Brene Brown
- *Ideas, Influence, and Income: Write a Book, Build Your Brand, and Lead Your Industry* by Tanya Hall
- *Authority: Become an Expert, Build a Following, and Gain Financial Independence* by Nathan Barry

LIST YOUR CONCEPTS

Determine the five to eight key concepts readers need to know about the topic. Use this information to create a book outline to keep you focused and organized. Under each concept, write three questions you will answer for your audience.

First Action Item for Hour Three: Determine the five to eight concepts anyone needs to know about your book idea. Leave space to write three questions under each main concept. Determine the three most important questions that need to be answered for that key concept. The five to eight concepts become the book chapters and the answers to the questions inside the chapters provide the content for each chapter.

Determine three questions that need to be addressed or answered under each main statement. Put the key concepts and questions into a logical order so the outline can easily be turned into a Table of Contents at a later time. This will make it easier for you to write to each idea.

Second Action Item: Use the draft outline you just created and refine it one last time before you begin the writing process. We have provided a Revised Outline format to allow you to refine your ideas.

BOOK OUTLINE INSTRUCTIONS *

*This expands on the action items for this hour

1. Select five to eight key concepts or key ideas you feel are important to include in your book, to cover the topic at the depth you choose. To help you determine this, think about who your audience is, how readers will use your book, and how *you* want to share your expertise to entertain, inform, or help others expand their perspective on your topic.

2. Write three questions for each concept that will explain that concept. Be specific. Here are some example questions:

- What is my unique concept?
- Why is this concept or idea important?
- How should the reader expect to benefit from it?
- What does the reader need to understand to benefit from it?

3. Add an Introduction (beginning) and Conclusion (end) in the outline. Don't worry much about writing your Introduction first unless you think it will help you to focus. The Introduction and the Conclusion are usually written or revisited *after* the rest of the writing is done.

DRAFT BOOK OUTLINE

This first draft outline can be handwritten and should take fewer than 20 minutes to create.

INTRODUCTION

CONCEPT 1:
    QUESTION: _____
    QUESTION: _____
    QUESTION: _____

CONCEPT 2:
    QUESTION: _____
    QUESTION: _____
    QUESTION: _____

CONCEPT 3:
    QUESTION: _____
    QUESTION: _____
    QUESTION: _____

CONCEPT 4:
    QUESTION: _____
    QUESTION: _____
    QUESTION: _____

CONCEPT 5:
    QUESTION: _____
    QUESTION: _____
    QUESTION: _____

CONCEPT 6:
    QUESTION: _____
    QUESTION: _____
    QUESTION: _____

CONCEPT 7:
    QUESTION: _____
    QUESTION: _____
    QUESTION: _____

CONCLUSION

REVISED BOOK OUTLINE

(You may want to type your updated outline into a Word document format so it's ready to go when you begin work on your manuscript.)

WORKING TITLE:

WORKING SUBTITLE:

INTRODUCTION

CHAPTER 1:

    QUESTION 1: _____

    QUESTION 2: _____

    QUESTION 3: _____

CHAPTER 2:

    QUESTION 1: _____

    QUESTION 2: _____

    QUESTION 3: _____

CHAPTER 3:

    QUESTION 1: _____

    QUESTION 2: _____

    QUESTION 3: _____

CHAPTER 4:

QUESTION 1: _____

QUESTION 2: _____

QUESTION 3: _____

CHAPTER 5:

QUESTION 1: _____

QUESTION 2: _____

QUESTION 3: _____

CHAPTER 6:

QUESTION 1: _____

QUESTION 2: _____

QUESTION 3: _____

CHAPTER 7:

QUESTION 1: _____

QUESTION 2: _____

QUESTION 3: _____

CHAPTER 8:

QUESTION 1: _____

QUESTION 2: _____

QUESTION 3: _____

CONCLUSION

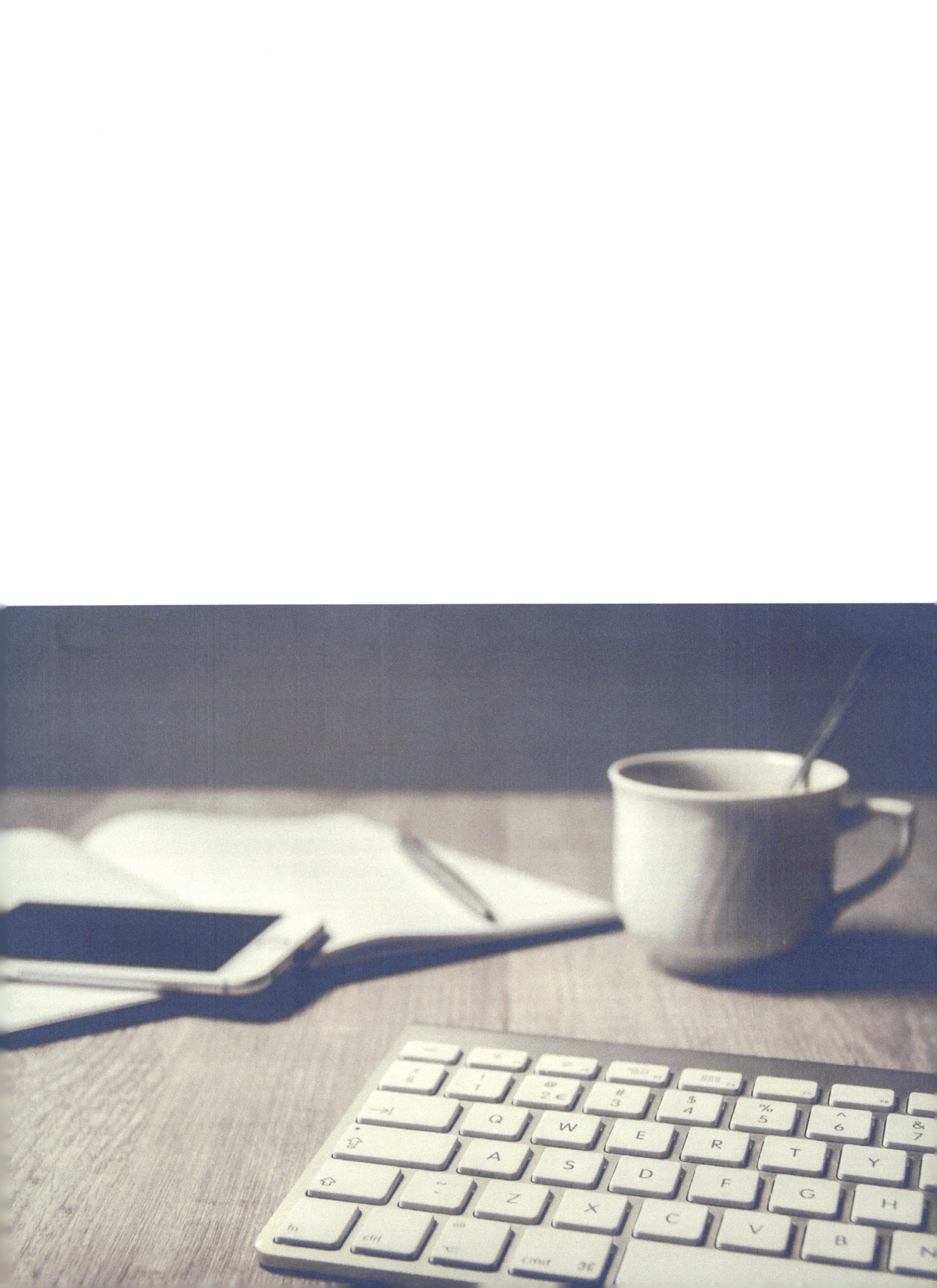

HOUR 4

WRITE! CHAPTERS 1 & 2

Using a timer, write for 10 minutes without editing on each of your questions under each concept (these will become chapters) in your outline.

First Action Item for Hour Four: Shut the door. Have someone watch your kids and pets. Determine that nothing short of a hurricane or a house fire will stop you from getting the content out of your head and into your computer during the next hour.

Here's the math: In this hour you can get two entire concepts (six questions) written. To believe this is true, try it with a timer. Write as fast as your fingers can type. It can be full sentences, lists, groups of ideas. Keep your fingers moving until the timer rings and move to the next question, even if you aren't done with the first question.

Writing without editing is the key to this process. Don't worry about punctuation, spelling, or anything else; just write. You only get 10 minutes to type as much content as you can on each key idea, focusing on answering the questions below the main idea. You will be amazed by what you can actually write down in this short time. Do this for each of your concepts. Then celebrate the accomplishment of getting great stuff out of your brain and onto "paper."

HOUR **5**

KEEP WRITING

Keep writing without editing in 10-minute intervals to create chapters 3 and 4. You'll be surprised, later in this process, how the writing you are doing now allows the book to take shape.

☐ **First Action Item for Hour Five:** Keep writing for 10 minutes on each question for two more key concepts—following the same format you used in the previous hour.

FOCUSED WRITING TIPS

FOR KEEPING THE MOMENTUM

Maintain focus on the question at hand. If this is hard, keep a notepad handy for writing down questions and ideas that pop into your head as you express your thoughts. If you think of more things to add, start a list but keep writing on your original topic.

WHEN YOU'RE STUCK

Skip that section and move on. You can come back after you've done some research or have taken a break. Listening to the timer tick has a way of ruining your focus.

When you go back to finish a skipped section, for inspiration look at what you've already written in the book or in a presentation or report you've created on a related topic.

HOUR 6

MAKING PROGRESS

Continue writing on two more concepts that will become chapters 5 and 6. As you write, keep in mind both the big picture message and your *why*—your reason for writing your book.

☐ **First Action Item for Hour Six:** Keep writing to answer every question/statement in your book outline. Think about your audience as you write: Are you offering them what they need to know?

HOUR 7

FINISH IT!

If you have more concepts (chapters), write to finish them. If you've covered them all, you have your first draft completed—congratulations! Spend this hour reviewing what you have written and fill in the gaps.

First Action Item for Hour Seven: Keep writing to fill in the gaps in your book outline. Think about the importance of each question as you write—is it the right question? Do you even need it? Is it in the right place? As your book comes together, you may start to see more clearly where things fit. But if you don't, don't worry. You'll have another chance when you work on the second draft—which is much easier to do than getting it out the first time.

Second Action Item: If your first draft is completed, review and make a list to fill in what's missing. These elements can be stories, statistics, and any other information you can add to support or expand on your message.

HOUR 8

REVIEW & COMPLETE YOUR FIRST DRAFT

If you're not done yet, keep writing. If you are, review to fill in the gaps so you answer every question/statement in your book outline. Start adding in stories and statistics to your manuscript.

☐ **First Action Item for Hour Eight:** If you have more than eight concepts to cover, this is where you'll spend hours over 12 . . . but you'll still complete the first draft of your book in fewer than 20 hours.

☐ **Second Action Item:** Add in stories and statistics. It may be easiest to record stories by audio, have them transcribed, and then have your editor help you fix them in your final manuscript.

If the actual writing isn't your thing, interview yourself or be interviewed by a friend, coach, or editor. Record directly to Garage Band on a Mac or the Rev app on your phone, where your recording can be sent directly to a transcription service.

☐ **Third Action Item:** Make sure your book outline is turning into a working book manuscript by organizing all your material into a chapter-like format. Grab content you have already created for speeches, blog posts, websites, or other content you have previously written, and add these into the appropriate areas of your manuscript.

Create an interview process if you feel you can speak to the topic better than you can write to it.

HOUR 9

FIND A GREAT EDITOR

Find a great editor—the right person to take your manuscript from good to outstanding and impactful. Find someone with passion, great skills, and who comes highly recommended by authors similar to you.

First Action Item for Hour Nine: Develop a plan to find an editor. Some of the best connections come from personal recommendations such as asking other authors, reading the acknowledgments from your favorite books, or calling a few publishing companies. LinkedIn Pro, local writers groups and organizations, plus online options such as Reedsy, Writers Digest, World Literary Café, and the Editorial Freelancers Association can also be a place to start.

☐ **Second Action Item:** Create a list of at least **three editors** to interview. Understand that you are looking for someone who will assist you in organizing your manuscript, give you excellent feedback, and who understands your writing style and message. It's a bonus if they have an interest in your topic and share your values.

Editors can and should make your best work better. Often editors may call themselves book coaches/consultants, content/developmental editors, line editors, copy editors, or proof-readers. No matter how you interpret them in terms of importance or price, all of these professional titles may fall in the scope of professional editors.

These terms can change or be interpreted differently, so ask which services are offered when you contact an editor. You may be able to find one editor to do most of the work except for the final proofread—which you should always have done by someone who has not worked with the manuscript prior to the proofreading stage. Some editors specialize in content development and will refer you elsewhere for line or copy editing.

For any new working relationship with an editor, request a sample edit. You should plan to pay for the sample edit. It's valuable to see if your editor is a good fit for the entire project.

☐ **Third Action Item:** Set up times to interview editors and determine which one you want to do a sample edit.

Once you've found an editor you like and they agree to do a sample edit, give them your outline and your first chapter or even the first 20 percent of your draft, to see if working together is a good fit. Understand you are agreeing to pay them for their work as you evaluate your working relationship. If you like what they do, you can continue working with them. If not, choose someone else to work with and avoid the challenge of partnering with someone who likely won't give you the desired end result—which is a book with the right message that you can be proud of.

An editor should help you be a better writer and help you express your ideas and messages in easy-to-understand language. If you don't see an improvement in the way the content "sounds" and communicates your message when you read the edited version, you may not have the right person.

WRITE THE INTRODUCTION

If the title and subtitle of the book are the most important words you write, the words in your Introduction are the next most important. Research and then write the Introduction for your book and turn it over to your editor.

First Action Item for Hour Ten: Be bold about telling why the material you have written will make a huge difference in the lives of those reading it. The Introduction needs to be clear and convincing to sell the reader on your point of view and the value of your book.

Use Introductions from books you have read—or want to read—as the model to writing your own great book Introduction.

Second Action Item: Go to the world's largest bookstore, Amazon, or grab books you own and read the introductions from authors you love. For me, it's Chris Guillebeau, Matthew Kelly, Ron Price, and others. Once you have researched how they capture your interest right from the beginning, use a similar style to create a compelling reason why readers must read your book.

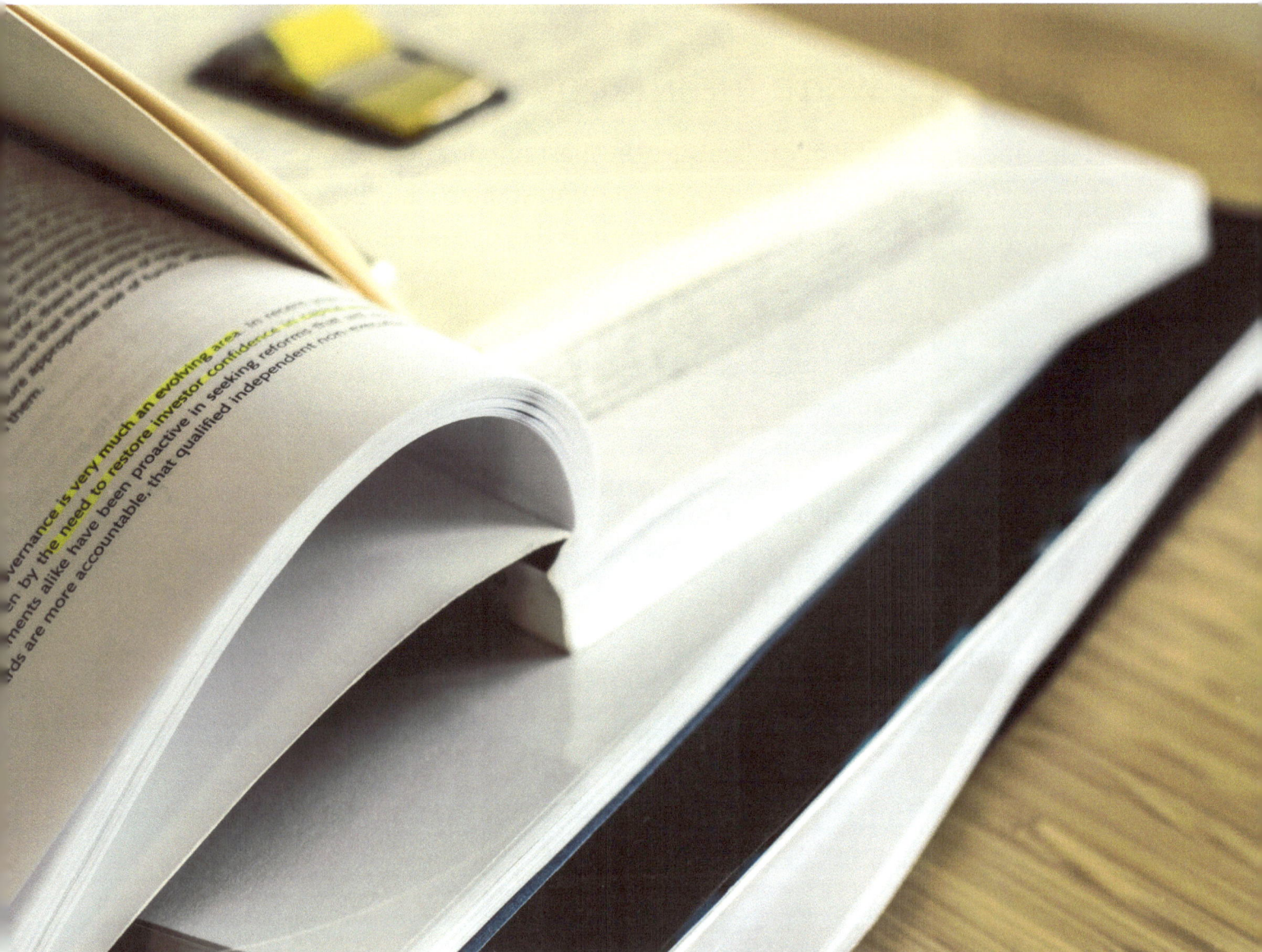

HOUR 11

WRITE BACK COVER COPY

Spend more time on your Introduction and then begin writing the back cover copy. The back cover copy consists of a sales headline, a compelling paragraph or two about how the book benefits the reader, a short author bio, categories for the book, and in many cases your top endorsements for the book.

☐ **First Action Item for Hour Eleven:** Spend a little more time polishing the book's Introduction. Give it to someone who knows your topic, and ask them if it's convincing and if it makes them want to know more. If it doesn't . . . consider doing some more research and even reading some of the top-selling books in your niche.

☐ **Second Action Item:** Start drafting the back cover copy for your book. Look at favorite and best-selling books in your genre to understand how those authors used what is inside their book to create the wording on the cover. Think keywords, keywords, keywords.

What are keywords? They are the search terms people type in the search bar when they are looking for something. So if you put the right keywords in your searchable content (title, subtitle, and back copy are the biggies), people will find your book. The right keywords drive sales and make the difference between a not-so-great book and a best seller.

Endorsements also can be an important part of the back cover. Don't worry about recruiting endorsers yet but leave room in the copy for one or two endorsements. You can even write down the general ideas of what you would like endorsers to say about your book.

ELEMENTS OF BACK COVER COPY

Write your copy following these four easy steps:

A. Write a compelling headline that is a call to action for the reader.

B. Write a paragraph that describes your book content (simply called a "book description").

C. List the benefits of the book—what the reader will get. Or, ask your endorsers to note the benefits of the book once they read a beta copy of your finished manuscript. You can place their endorsements on the cover.

D. Turn your "About the Author" content into a short author bio with three to four sentences about who you are and why you have the credibility to write the book. It can be difficult to write a polished bio for yourself. To get started, put together up to 10 major points about yourself and then hire a PR professional or your editor to compile it for you.

Back cover copy is what most readers use to help them decide if they should buy your book—so it is your primary marketing content. Back copy contains four elements:

- Headline (grabs readers' attention)
- Body (what readers will get)
- Endorsements (what you want people to say about your book)
- A short author bio (convinces readers of your credibility)

WRITE FRONT & BACK MATTER

Create the front and back matter for your book. Front matter includes the Copyright page, Dedication, Table of Contents, and can include a key quote for the book. Back matter includes Acknowledgements and About the Author, and may include References, an Index, or an Appendix.

First Action Item for Hour Twelve: Turn your book outline into a completed Table of Contents. The Table of Contents can be a powerful marketing tool if you choose chapter titles with keywords in mind. You do this by simply refining the concepts/chapter titles you wrote in your outline by using keywords wherever you can and making them intriguing—because you truly are using these to sell your book.

Because it's a part of both marketing and the book content, another significant piece to consider is the Foreword. The Foreword is written in addition to the introduction, usually by an influential person who can personally vouch for your credibility. If you want to include a Foreword, start thinking about who should write it and begin recruiting that person early. You want to allow time to include the Foreword content and that person's name in your final book production.

If you want both results and relationships in your leadership style, this is your guide.

Leadership doesn't have to be complicated or overwhelming but as a leader, you may feel it is both. *The Square and the Triangle* is the model to clear the clutter.

To be a leader, you need to do two things: build relationships with people and get results. Simple yet powerful.

The Square and the Triangle approach uses **two competencies** to cover the entire leadership landscape:

☐ The Square - Relationships
△ The Triangle - Results

You are naturally better at either relationships or results in leadership. Once you know that, you can pick up what you need to know to get the job done—and build on it to create your own style for impact, clarity, and less stress, every day.

"Being a better leader really can be simple. Mark Stevens has devised a fabulous way to be the leader you were meant to be."
LaVay Lauter, Vice President, Director of Talent Development, Baird

MARK STEVENS is the founder and CEO of The Square and the Triangle Coaching and HR Consulting, Inc. He has served in senior level roles in healthcare, biomedical/pharmaceutical, logistics, and retail. Mark is passionate about leadership development and has taught the Square and Triangle concepts to hundreds of teams, leaders, and organizations. His focus on simplicity has helped leaders achieve success quickly and sustainably. He lives in the Pacific Northwest with his wife, Shelly, her three children, and enough pets to keep them energized for whatever comes their way. He loves cycling and teaching fly fishing in the best rivers throughout the western U.S.

TheSquareandtheTriangle.com

$22.95

ISBN 978-1-61206-147-4
9 781612 061474
52295 >

ALOHA PUBLISHING

Leadership
Corporate Training
Human Resources

FRONT MATTER CHECKLIST

- Endorsements (optional)
- Title Page (title, subtitle and the way you want the author name written)
- Copyright page
- Dedication
- Table of Contents (TOC) from your book outline
- Foreword (optional)

Second Action Item: Write a Dedication. You can dedicate the book to the one or two people who have inspired or supported your writing. Or, you can dedicate it to the audience for whom the book is intended.

BACK MATTER CHECKLIST

- References/Endnotes (optional)
- Appendix (optional)
- Index (optional)
- Acknowledgments
- About the Author(s)

Third Action Item: Start writing the Acknowledgments section as a list of credits to those who helped you with your project. Use your professional bio to draft your About the Author section. Your editor can help you with each of these sections.

WHAT'S NEXT?

When you finish this process, you will have the first draft manuscript—the most difficult part of writing a book—completed. Congratulations!

Once you have found your editor, wait for the edited version before revisiting your work. You may be surprised by how much your book is improved by the editing process, but that process will usually include returning the manuscript to you for further development. So get ready for that next round of writing when you will refine and clarify your message and add supporting content such as stories, data, and graphics.

If you have not utilized a book coach, book publishing professional, or a partner publisher to help you in the writing process, you may want to consider finding one to help you design and publish the book. These professionals can help you produce a book that clearly shows your expertise and compares to the best books available in the marketplace. Writing a great book but then having a bad cover or poor printing will be very evident and crush the book's ability to showcase your talent and appeal to your niche.

Get personal recommendations from other authors about the book production professionals they use independently or through their publisher in the areas of cover and interior design, proofreading, and ebook conversion.

And send me a copy when your book is complete. I will celebrate with you!

25

twenty five

Absolutely ESSENTIAL

Things You Need to Know About

Writing and Publishing a BOOK

An Integrative Kickstart for Writing and Selling Your Book with Less Effort and More Impact

MARYANNA YOUNG

Author and Publisher

RESOURCES

25 Absolutely Essential Things for Writing and Publishing a Book by Maryanna Young – An overall, easy-to-follow guide book for understanding how to write and publish with less stress.

Authorfriendly.com – Great site by publishing expert Carla King. Her courses provide excellent information.

Authority: Become an Expert, Build a Following and Gain Financial Independence by Nathan Barry – This book (or the audio version) is a great resource to help you understand the writing process. In one year, this author made over $250,000 by writing and publishing three books.

Booklaunch.com – Tim Grahl's (*Your First 1000 Copies*) website is primarily dedicated to promoting a self-published or independently published work of nonfiction. Tim also runs a great podcast.

Bowker.com – The resource for independent authors to obtain ISBNs (International Standard Book Numbers). Also see MyIdentifiers.com.

FusionCW.com – Fusion Creative Works is an excellent resource for cover design, interior layout, ebooks, and website. I personally have been working with this company for more than six years.

Goinswriter.com – This is Jeff Goins' website, which is all about helping people become better writers. He created a challenge called "My 500 Words," designed to develop a healthy habit of writing.

Ibpa-online.org – This is the Independent Book Publishers Association. There is a small membership fee; however, the resources you receive include a monthly magazine and discounts to numerous valuable resources.

Ideas, Influence, and Income: Write a Book, Build Your Brand, and Lead Your Industry by Tanya Hall – This book offers a tremendous amount of knowledge about every step of publishing a nonfiction book. Tanya Hall is the CEO of Greenleaf Book Group. This book focuses on the benefits of writing a book—what it can do for you personally and professionally.

NathanBarry.com – Great site for encouragement to write 1000 words a day (see his blog, "One Year After Quitting My Job"). Nathan started as an author and created an awesome company for bloggers and creators called *ConvertKit*.

NonfictionAuthorsAssociation.com – There is a little bit of everything regarding the world of nonfiction publishing on this site. Writing, production, and promotion; as well as templates, checklists, and worksheets are all available here.

NonfictionWritersConference.com – A two-day remote event dedicated to helping nonfiction authors write, publish, and promote their work.

NorthAmericanBookAwards.com – Authors send their books for consideration, and NABA decides whether your book qualifies for a Gold, Silver, or Bronze medal. Awards can be a great way to appeal to potential readers.

Penzu.com – Penzu is a website that allows you to digitize your journaling. It is completely private and offers options to customize your journal. Best of all, you can have it wherever you go.

SeanWes.com – This website is built around a challenge called "30 Days to Better Writing." Sean Wes has a philosophy that everything we want to accomplish will include writing, so we should all be practicing it to refine the craft.

SmartPassiveIncome.com – Pat Flynn, the creator of this site, is an entrepreneur and author. This website is not focused on writing and publishing, but it does have some great information on online business, podcasting, and blogging. Check out the article, "How to Write a Book: The Secret to a Super-Fast First Draft."

ACKNOWLEDGMENTS

The 12-hour process came from working with hundreds of individuals who were writing books through workshops and private coaching over more than a decade. Your input resulted in this book. The first version of this book came out in 2013 and with this update we have intended to keep it simple.

My heartfelt thanks to Hannah Rhinehart for her expertise, support, and friendship in the making of the first version of this book. She helped me in too many ways to count.

Anna McHargue, Freddy Betzold, and Jennifer Regner made real contributions to this updated version and gave me great ideas to make this a truly useful book.

Thanks to Rachel, Jessi, and Shiloh of Fusion Creative Works for helping me make yet another beautiful book. You make it all look easy.

Many thanks to all of the Aloha authors who have worked with us over the years. You have proven that this method works.

ABOUT THE AUTHOR

Maryanna Young excels at forging new paths and has specialized at learning to make a living by doing what she loves. As a student athlete, she started a company that ran sporting events and created work opportunities for other students, as a means of paying their college tuition and coming out of college debt-free. While at Oral Roberts University, she worked with the women's basketball team and later became Assistant Coach for Cross-Country Track and Field.

She trained and competed as a member of the USA Korfball team and played on the World Cup Team in 1983, followed by a career in personal training that brought her back to her hometown of Boise, Idaho. In the role of CEO of Fitness Management Group, she was one of the first female sports agents in Olympic and Paralympic sports. She developed the concept for and co-founded the Idaho Women's Fitness Celebration, one of the largest sporting events for women in the United States and was named Race Director of the Year by USA Running.

She founded Aloha Publishing in 2004 to offer anyone with a powerful idea the opportunity to write and publish a high-quality book. Since that time, the team at Aloha has helped hundreds of writers and non-writers become authors with the essence of Aloha—love, joy, compassion, and giving. The Hawaiian word Aloha means "breath of God."

Maryanna is a coffee lover and visionary who enjoys the mountains and rivers of Idaho and the beaches and sunsets of Maui, where she has traveled once or twice a year for more than three decades.

She would love to connect with you about your business and book ideas. Reach out to her at maryannayoung@gmail.com

www.ingramcontent.com/pod-product-compliance
Lightning Source LLC
Chambersburg PA
CBHW060843200326
41521CB00003BB/163